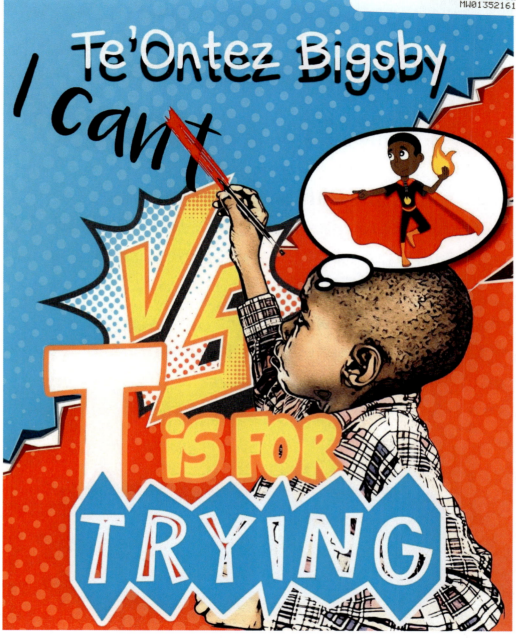

Dedicated to:

Every child who struggles while trying to focus. Every child who has a hard time sitting still for too long. Every parent who fights this battle day in and day out. Every child who has to take medicine and struggles with wondering if something is wrong with them on the inside.

I want you to know that you are not different. You are just eager to get up and go. You enjoy being busy. Take I can't out of your vocabulary and know that you can because you tried!!! No matter what, always give it your best!!!

T is for Trying...

Te'Ontez Bigsby

Guided by: Danielle Bigsby

Cover Design: Navi' Robins and Northshore Graphics

Publisher: Royal 4 Publishing Presents

In math, I draw a number line to help me solve problems.

In science, I gather research and use my reading skills to understand. I also ask my teachers for help if I can't seem to get the hang of it.

Reading isn't easy for me. It's hard for me to slow down. Chapter books make me take my time and I don't like to do that. Even though it's hard for me, I still try to ask for help and do my best.

Now football, that's fun! I get to tackle and hit people but not get in trouble. I also get to wear a bunch of equipment. I love to run around and play plus with football I get to stretch my legs. It gives me so much energy. I love it when my mom watches me during a game. I love making her proud. The only time that I don't like football is when I don't get to play because I got in trouble in school.

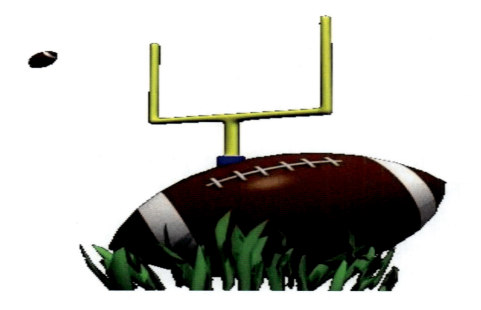

11

Basketball is different from football. You have to dribble the ball and be quick on your feet. I love shooting the ball through the hoop. I like when the ball goes in the hoop. It takes a lot of practice to be really good at basketball. When you don't give it your all, it makes it hard to be at your best.

Combing my hair used to be so hard for me. I didn't get to move when my mom was combing it and that always made me mad. I used to cry and fight. I would beg her to stop but she never did. I could've been a big boy and just let her comb it but it hurt too much. So instead of getting it combed, I just let her get it cut. In my eyes, that made me a big boy.

The ride to school is always a hard one for me. I don't do so well on the school bus. I have a lot of problems there. I try to be good but I can't seem to sit still for too long no matter how hard I try. Sometimes people bother me and end up making me mad. I usually get upset and end up doing things that get me in trouble. Whenever I get in trouble, I get sad because I was trying to be good. I also get sad when they won't let me ride the bus because I'm in trouble so I try my best to behave. This is so hard for me but I won't give up and I won't stop trying to be good.

School is fun for me most of the time but sometimes I have a hard time. I struggle so hard sitting still but I try my best. Class is so long and sometimes I just don't understand some things. I distract my friends when I can't seem to learn. My teachers try to help me and keep me out of trouble but sometimes I just can't seem to help it. I really enjoy learning because it's fun. Although it's difficult to focus, I won't give up!

At home, things are quite different. I have to follow my mom's directions and do just as she says but I don't like. She always tells me not to talk back but sometimes I just get so mad. When I get in trouble, I usually get put on punishment. No football, no basketball or no TV at all. Fun stuff is taken away completely when I don't follow the rules at home. I don't like being on punishment and makes me angry when my mom takes things away. So I try my best to follow her directions the first time.

Sharing my feelings is something that I'm not so good at. I don't like telling others my feelings because I don't want others to know just how I feel on the inside. I try my best to my mom though because I know that she needs to know. I trust her and my big sister Eniyah with my feelings. I also draw pictures to show others how I feel sometimes. Writing them down sometimes helps me too. I'm still trying my best to communicate how I feel.

No matter how hard things may get, I won't ever quit and you shouldn't either! No matter how hard it gets, you still have to try your best and never give up!

Author Bio:

Te'Ontez Bigsby is a nine-year-old energetic child. He suffers from ADHD but loves to helps others. Although his attention span is short, he gives it his all while never giving up. His goal in life is to become a better person and help other children. His heart is bigger than life and showcases his big personality. This is his first book of many to come.

Danielle Bigsby is the CEO of Royal 4 Publishing Presents as well as an author on the roster. She has several literary works under her belt and truly believes in giving back. It is easy to see where her son, Te'Ontez gets his big heart. Her only goal with her literary endeavors is to empower and inspire others to make their lives count for something.

Made in the USA
Monee, IL
30 January 2021